The Great British Cake Baking book

Chef: Amelia George

For free pdf books contact us;

mail to: kevinbookpublication@gmail.com

There's nothing more comforting than indulging in a piece of homemade cake paired with a piping hot cup of coffee or tea. Sounds rejuvenating. Well, here's some simple and quick homemade cake recipes, which you can prepare at home without putting in much efforts. If you want to prepare a cake for your dear ones, but you don't have a microwave, in that case, just stop worrying and try these amazing easy Cake recipes prepared using a pressure cooker.

An ideal dessert for birthdays and anniversaries, this homemade cake recipe is popular for its fresh and fluffy base. Made with all purpose flour, eggs and vanilla essence, this easy vegetarian recipe can also be used as a base for making other cake variations. It might look difficult to prepare this cake, especially, in a similar way prepared by connoisseurs.

You will be surprised to know that it is the easiest cake that can be prepared in just a few minutes using some simple tips and tricks. Also, if you have sudden guests dropping by and you feel too lazy to make something exotic and elaborate, then this cake can serve as a perfect high-tea snack. The best thing about preparing this cake at home is that you can control the quality of ingredients used.

Moreover, you can also add ingredients as per your plate preference, for instance, if you are found of exotic dried fruits and nuts, you can dry roast and add it to the batter, this will certainly accentuate the taste of this Cake recipes. So, try this simple yet delectable cake recipes, and delve into the flavors of this delightful cakes.

- It is good for our heart and circulation of blood.

- Consumption of chocolate lowers the risk of strokes.

- It contains minerals like selenium, potassium, zinc that are good for our health.

- Cocoa has a plus point that it increases the level of cholesterol that is good for health and it reduces the level of cholesterol.

- Dark chocolate contains flavone's, which can protect our skin from sun damage.

- The chocolate cake can help you to lose your weight.

- According to research, pregnant ladies should eat chocolate cake because it reduces the level of stress and the babies.

RECIPES

Classic Christmas Cake

Ingredients:

- *4 tablespoon grated, soaked overnight orange zest*

- *100 gm brown sugar*

- *37 1/2 gm honey*

- *1 pinch clove powder*

- *1 large baking tin*

- *60 gm unsalted butter*

- *120 gm all-purpose flour*

- *1 teaspoon 5 spice powder*

- *100 gm chopped, soaked overnight walnuts*

The Main Dish

- *180 gm soaked overnight raisins*

- *80 gm chopped, soaked overnight apricots*
- *80 ml ice wine*
- *150 gm soaked overnight sultanas*
- *80 gm chopped, soaked overnight dried figs*
- *1 beaten egg*

Classic Christmas Cake:

Step 1

For making this yummy cake recipe, take a large bowl Place all the dried fruit in a large bowl then stir in the grated orange zest and juice, pour ice wine over them. Cover and leave to soak overnight.

Step 2

Preheat the oven to 150°C, gas mark 2. Grease and line the base and sides of a 23cm-round or 20cm-square cake tin with baking parchment so it stands 5cm above the top. Use string to tie a double thickness of baking parchment around the outside of the tin. This will help prevent the cake drying out during cooking.

Step 3

Beat together the butter and sugar until pale and fluffy. Gradually beat in the egg, a little at a time. If the mixture begins to curdle, add a spoonful of flour with the last few additions of egg.

Step 4

Now add all purpose flour with clove powder and mixed spices, and finally add in the soaked dry fruits. Mix them well. Take a baking tin lined with parchment paper and grease it with a little butter, then transfer the mixture in it.

Step 5

Stand the tin on a tray and bake for 3 to 4 hours until cooked through, covering the top of the cake with foil if it starts to over-brown. To check that the cake is cooked, insert a skewer into its Centre, If the skewer comes out clean the cake is cooked.

Step 6

When the cake is baked, remove the tray and cool down. You can store this cake for a few days in an airtight container. When you want to serve, cut thick slices and serve.

Homemade Cake Recipe

Ingredients:

- cup all-purpose flour
- 1 and 1/3 teaspoon baking soda
- 1 and 1/4 egg
- 1 and 1/3 teaspoon vanilla essence
- 1 and 1/3 cup powdered sugar
- 2/3 cup butter
- 1 and 1/3 cup milk

Homemade Cake:

Step 1- Cream together butter sugar and then blend with beaten eggs

If you think you can never make that perfect sponge cake, then try this simple recipe and you surely become a master in rolling out the perfect homemade cake. It is a simple recipe and you can begin by mixing sugar and then butter together. Whisk well until light and fluffy. Then, take a manual whisker or a fork, if you do not have one. Even electrical blenders are good. Once done, add the beaten eggs and blend well. Beat further so that the mixture gets a light, white appearance.

Step 2- Mix together flour mix and beaten eggs

Sift together the all-purpose flour and baking soda. It is done to evenly distribute the baking soda in flour. Gradually, add this to the egg mixture. If required, add a little milk and mix till the batter is fluffy and soft. Add vanilla essence and blend well. Vanilla essence is important to camouflage the smell of eggs.

Step 3- Cook the cake as per your convenience

Sprinkle some Maida on a greased baking tin. It will prevent sticking of the cake to the base, you can also line it with a butter paper. Pour the prepared mixture into the tin and place it in a pressure cooker. Do not add water in the cooker and ensure that the tin does not touch the base of cooker. You can keep the baking dish on an inverted steel plate. Increase the flame and pressure cook for two minutes. Now remove the whistle and cook on low flame for 35-40 minutes. If you are using an electric oven, cook at 180° for 30-35 minutes.

Step 4- Check with a knife or skewer if it is cooked and serve

Insert a knife or a metal skewer into the cake and if it comes out clean, then the cake is ready to devour in. Remove from the oven/cooker and allow to cool on a wire rack.

Microwave Chocolate Cake

Ingredients:

- *4 tablespoon cooking chocolate*
- *4 tablespoon Brown sugar*
- *1 egg*
- *1 teaspoon cocoa powder*
- *1 tablespoon icing sugar*
- *4 tablespoon butter*
- *4 tablespoons all-purpose flour*
- *1/4 teaspoon vanilla extract*
- *1 pinch salt*

Microwave Chocolate cake

Step 1

Grease a 22cm silicone microwaveable cake pan with a little oil and place a circle of baking parchment in the bottom. Then add the chocolate, butter and sugar into a glass bowl.

Step 2

Place it in the microwave and cook on high power for 30 seconds or until melted.

Step 3

Add the remaining ingredients and mix the ingredients well.

Step 4

Transfer it in the cake tin and microwave for 5 min or until just set. Allow it to cool.

Step 5

Sprinkle cocoa powder (or icing sugar) on top and serve.

Chocolate Brownie Cake

Ingredients:

- *3 and 1/4 tablespoon all-purpose flour*
- *1/3 cup and 1 tablespoon unsalted butter*
- *1/3 cup and 1 tablespoon caster sugar*
- *1 and 1/4 egg whites*
- *1/3 cup and 2 and 1/2 tablespoon dark chocolate*
- *1 and 1/2 tablespoon pecan*
- *icing sugar as required*
- *1 and 1/4 egg yolk*

Chocolate Brownie Cake

Step 1

To prepare this yummy cake recipe, preheat the oven at 180° Celsius. Then, take a medium cake tin and grease it with some unsalted butter. After greasing, line it with grease proof paper.

Step 2

Next, put a large heavy-bottomed pan over low to medium flame then cut medium chunks of chocolate in it. Add the remaining butter along with sugar in the same pan and let the chocolate melt in heat gradually, stirring occasionally. Once done, keep it aside to cool. (Note: You can melt the chocolate in microwave as well.

Step 3

Now, add egg yolks into the melted chocolate mixture and whisk well. Then, add all purpose flour in the mixture along with the pecan nuts and the remaining chocolate. (Note: You can also go for walnuts along with pecan nuts in this recipe.

Step 4

In another bowl, add the egg whites and beat them well using an electric beater until they form soft peaks. Once done, gently fold the egg whites into the chocolate mixture.

Step 5

Your cake batter is ready, pour it into the prepared tin. Place the cake tin in the preheated oven and let the cake bake in the Centre of the oven for about 35-40 minutes. Make sure that the top of your cake is crusty.

Step 6

Once the cake is baked well, let it cool and then using a knife take it out of the cake tin. Use a little icing sugar for dusting on the top and serve it warm. Enjoy with vanilla ice cream or chocolate sauce.

Black Forest Cake

Ingredients:

- *1 cup all-purpose flour*
- *1/2 cup sugar*
- *1/4 cup butter*
- *225 grams whipped cream*
- *1/4 cup sugar*
- *2 tablespoon cherry juice*
- *1/2 cup cocoa powder*
- *1 teaspoon baking powder*
- *2 egg*
- *200 grams cooking chocolate*
- *1/4 cup Water, 1 cup cherry jam*

Black Forest Cake:

Step 1

Mix together flour, baking powder and cocoa. In a bowl, beat the butter and sugar till creamy. Add eggs and beat till frothy. Fold in the dry ingredients.

Step 3

Whisk well for a min. This measurement is for 1 chocolate cake. We will need 2 cakes like this. So repeat this process for the 2nd cake.

Step 4

Pour each separately prepared batter into a separate greased pan. Bake both cakes in a 350F pre-heated oven for 30-35 mines. Remove the baked cakes from the oven and cool on a cooling rack.

Step 5

Meanwhile prepare a sugar syrup with 1/2 cup sugar and 1/4 cup water. When the sugar syrup is ready, let it cool and add cherry juice.

Step 6

Process 3-4 tbsp. of cherry jam in a food processor till the filling is slightly crushed. Save the rest of the cherry jam as filling for later.

Step 7

Now, to assemble the cake, place the 1st layer of the chocolate cake on a platter. Drizzle with the cherry flavored sugar syrup till the cake is moist.

Step 8

Spread with one layer of whipped cream. Top with the processed cherry jam filling.

Step 9

Now place the 2nd layer of the cake. Spoon whipped cream onto the top layer and frost the cake using a spatula.

Step 10

After the whole cake has been frosted with the whipped topping, spoon some cherry jam onto the middle of the top cake layer.

Step 11

Now decorate around the cherry filling using a piping bag filled with whipped topping fitted with a star shaped nozzle.

Step 12

Grate the chocolate bar to get chocolate shavings. Sprinkle this on the sides of the cake.

Step 13

Decorate the lower part of the cake with the star nozzle piping bag. Refrigerate till you are ready to cut it. Enjoy.

Banana Cake

Ingredients:

- *3/4 cup and 1 and 1/4 tablespoon all-purpose flour*

- *50 milliliters buttermilk*

- *2 and 3/4 tablespoon unsalted butter*

- *3/4 egg*

- *salt as required*

- *1 and 1/4 banana*

- *4 tablespoon brown sugar*

- *1/3 cup sugar*

- *1/3 tablespoon baking soda*

- *2 and 3/4 tablespoon walnuts*

Banana Cake

Step 1

To prepare this delicious tea cake recipe, preheat the oven at 180°Celsius. For making these cakes, you would need two 8-inch round pans. Take a little butter and grease them well with it. Once done, take a little dry flour and dust the pans with it.

Step 2

Next, you need to prepare the cake batter. For the same, sift together all purpose flour, salt, and baking soda in a large bowl. Keep this bowl aside until required.

Step 3

Now, take a large bowl and add unsalted butter in it along with brown sugar and white sugar. Using an electric beater, beat together all the ingredients until light and fluffy. (Note: If you have light brown sugar, use that.

Step 4

Once the butter-sugar mixture is creamy, add egg, one at a time and the beat well once again. Afterwards, peel the bananas and add them to the mixture as well. Beat once again.

Step 5

Now, add the flour mixture in this bowl along with buttermilk, and beat one last time to make the batter. Make sure that no lumps are remaining. Once the batter is ready, add chopped walnuts in it and stir using a spoon.

Step 6

Transfer this cake batter in the greased pans and put them in the preheated ovens. Bake these banana cakes for about 20-30 minutes. After half an hour, take out the pans and let the cake cool at room temperature. Serve warm with tea/ coffee, as you like.

Carrot Cake

Ingredients:

- *250 gm pureed, washed & dried carrot*
- *300 gm sugar*
- *4 egg*
- *250 gm all-purpose flour*
- *1 teaspoon baking powder*
- *2 teaspoon powdered cinnamon*

Garnishing

- *50 gm chopped walnuts*

The Main Dish

- *300 ml corn oil*

For Toppings

- *100 gm unsalted butter*

- *2 cup powdered sugar*

- *100 gm cream cheese*

- *1 teaspoon vanilla extract*

Carrot Cake:

Step 1

To prepare this healthy cake recipe, preheat the oven at 180° Celsius. Meanwhile, wash the carrots under cold running water. Then wipe them with a cloth. Peel the carrots and grind them to a fine puree.

Step 2

Then take a glass bowl and mix all purpose flour, baking powder, cinnamon powder and walnuts in it. In an another bowl, break the eggs, add the sugar and whisk well. Once done, transfer this to the flour mixture along with corn oil and previously prepared carrot puree. Mix the ingredients properly.

Step 3

Then, transfer this mixture to a greased cake pan lined with parchment paper and place it into the preheated oven. Bake the cake batter for 20 to 25 minutes. Meanwhile, prepare the cream cheese frosting by beating the butter and cream together in a glass bowl.

Step 4

Add sugar and vanilla extract in it. Continue to beat until smooth and creamy. Once the cake has been properly baked, remove it and allow it to cool down. Spread the cream cheese frosting on top of the cake and garnish with walnuts. Serve this to your family and friend.

Chocolate Fudge with Salted Caramel Crumble

Ingredients:

- *1/2 cup all-purpose flour*
- *1/2 teaspoon baking soda*
- *100 gm chopped cooking chocolate*
- *1 cup sugar*
- *1/2 cup ground, peeled almonds*
- *1 teaspoon baking powder*
- *1/4 cup cocoa powder*

- *2 beaten egg*
- *1 cup butter*
- *1 teaspoon sea salt*

For The Main Dish

- *3 tablespoons all-purpose flour*
- *3 tablespoon sugar*
- *2 tablespoon butter*

For Toppings
- *4 tablespoon whipped cream*

Chocolate Fudge with Salted Caramel Crumble

Step 1

To prepare the fudge, pre-heat the oven at 180° Celsius. On the other hand, sift the flour, baking powder, baking soda and cocoa powder into a bowl.

Step 2

Melt the chocolate in the top of a double boiler and set aside. Keep warm.

Step 3

Whisk the eggs and sugar in another bowl till light and fluffy. Add the butter in it and beat till well incorporated.

Step 4

Gently mix in the melted chocolate. Fold in the flour mixture to make a smooth batter.

Step 5

Pour the batter into a lightly greased 8-inch cake mound.

Step 6

Bake in the Centre of a pre-heated oven for about 20-25 minutes, till a skewer inserted into the Centre of the cake comes out clean.

Step 7

Remove from the oven, but do not switch off the oven.

Step 8

For the crumble, put all the ingredients except the salt into a bowl and mix lightly till they resemble breadcrumbs.

Step 9

Spoon it into a cake mound and put it in the Centre of the oven for 15 minutes till golden brown.

Step 10

Remove and set aside to cool. Sprinkle the salt on top.

Step 11

Slice the chocolate fudge and serve it with cream and salted caramel crumble.

Chocolate Tart

Ingredients:

- *1 1/2 cup all-purpose flour*
- *1 cup butter*
- *1/2 cup powdered sugar*
- *10 gm baking powder*

Filling

- *500 gm compound chocolate*
- *1 egg*
- *1/4 cup sugar*
- *0 salt as required*

- *100 gm butter*
- *1/2 cup heavy cream*
- *4 drops vanilla extract*

Garnishing

- *1 teaspoon cocoa powder*
- *2 tablespoon chopped walnuts*
- *1 teaspoon icing sugar*

Chocolate Tart

Step 1

To prepare the crust of the tart, combine together the powdered sugar (confectioners' sugar), baking powder, all purpose flour and butter in a food processor, and process until the mixture forms a ball. Alternatively, you can also crumble the mixture and form a dough.

Step 2

Now with the help of your fingers, press the dough into a 12-inch tart pan with a removable bottom. Make sure that the crust is pushed into the indentations on the sides.

Step 3

Pat the dough until it's even and bake for 10 to 12 minutes on 180°C or until it gets light brown in color. The tart crust is ready. Set aside to cool.

Step 4

Now, to prepare the filling of the tart, melt compound dark chocolate and butter in a heavy saucepan over low flame, stirring until smooth. Then remove from flame and cool the mixture for 5 minutes.

Step 5

In a large bowl, whisk together egg, heavy cream, sugar, salt, and vanilla extract. Then whisk the chocolate mixture into egg mixture until well combined.

Step 6

Pour this filling into cooled crust and rap the pan once on the counter to eliminate any air bubbles.

Step 7

Bake until the filling is set and slightly puffed (1-inch from edge). Make sure that the center trembles a bit when pan is gently shaken for about 20 to 25 minutes (center will continue to set as it cools).

Step 8

De-mound the tart and cool it completely. Garnish the tarts with chopped walnuts. Sprinkle some cocoa powder and icing sugar over it and serve. Enjoy the delicious tart recipe.

Banana and Chocolate Chip Muffins

Ingredients:

- 1 cup all-purpose flour
- 2 banana
- 1 egg
- 1/4 cup unsalted butter
- 50 ml milk
- 1 teaspoon baking powder
- 100 gm chocolate chips
- 100 gm powdered sugar
- 1 pinch salt

Banana and Chocolate Chip Muffins:

Step 1

To prepare this easy recipe, preheat the oven at 180° Celsius. Take foil muffin liners and cover the required muffin cups with it. Once done, take a large bowl and mix together all purpose flour, baking powder, powdered sugar and salt.

Step 2

Once done, peel the bananas and mash them in a bowl. Then, take a medium bowl and crack open the egg in it. Next, add milk along with unsalted butter in it and of course mashed banana. Beat well so that all the ingredients are mixed together.

Step 3

Afterwards, fold the dry ingredients into the wet ones until they are blended well. Make sure that you do not over mix them. Finally, add the chocolate chips in the muffin batter.

Step 4

Using a spoon, pour this batter in the prepared muffin cups. Make sure that you fill only till 3/4 as the muffin will get fluffy. Place these muffin cups in a baking tray and put it inside the preheated oven. Bake the muffins until the top is pale golden for about 25-30 min.

Step 5

Once done, transfer the muffins to rack and let them cool at room temperature. Serve fresh with your favorite tea/coffee

Birthday Cake

Ingredients:

- 2 cup all-purpose flour

- 1 teaspoon baking soda

- 2 teaspoons 5 spice powder

- 100 ml black coffee

- 1 teaspoon vanilla extract

- 1 1/2 cup powdered sugar

- 1 1/2 cup dark chocolate

- 1/2 teaspoon salt

- 1 egg

- *100 ml buttermilk*

- *4 tablespoon chocolate chips*

- *1 teaspoon baking powder*

Birthday Cake:

Step 1

To prepare this easy cake recipe, take a large bowl and sift together all purpose flour, baking powder, baking soda, salt and 5-spice powder.

Step 2

Next, using the double-boiler method, melt the dark chocolate. Once the chocolate is melted, add black coffee in it and stir to mix well. Quickly add the buttermilk and vanilla extract in this mixture and stir again so that all the ingredients are mixed well. Afterwards, turn off the flame and put aside the bowl of coffee-chocolate mixture.

Step 3

Now, crack open the egg in a large bowl and add powdered sugar in it. Using an electric beater, beat them well until soft peaks form.

Step 4

In this egg mix bowl, add the chocolate mixture and beat whisk once. Next, add the flour mixture in it and whisk again until well blended. Make sure that the cake batter is smooth and there are no lumps remaining. Add chocolate chips in this cake batter and mix once again.

Step 5

Finally, take a cake tin and grease it with a little butter or simply use a butter paper. Transfer the cake batter in the cake tin and place inside a preheated oven at 180° Celsius. Bake the cake for 30-40 min. Check after half an hour if the cake is baked well. (Note: Use a skewer to check if the cake is baked or not. If it comes out clean then it is baked, else you will have to bake it for another 10-15 min.)

Step 6

Once the cake is baked, remove from the oven and let it cool at room temperature. Once cooled, put inside the refrigerator for chilling. Cut into slices when its chilled and serve. (Tip: You can garnish the cake, as you like.)

Vanilla Cake Recipe

Ingredients:

- 1 cup all-purpose flour
- 1/3 teaspoon baking powder
- 2 cup egg
- 1/2 teaspoon baking soda
- 20 gm Raisins
- 3/4 cup powdered sugar
- 1/4 cup milk
- 3/4 cup butter
- 1/2 teaspoon vanilla essence
- 20 cashews
- 1 pinch salt

Vanilla Cake Recipe:

Step 1

Vanilla Cake is one of the simplest cake recipe, which can be prepared with some easily available ingredients in your kitchen. To begin with take a large bowl and mix all purpose flour (Maida), salt, baking powder and baking soda in a bowl. Then, sift 3 times and keep it aside.

Step 2

Take another bowl and beat eggs, till it forms a thick foam, then add powdered sugar. If you want to make it healthy, you can replace regular sugar and use stevia or sugar-free.

Step 3

It will give the cake a sweet taste without adding on to the calories. Then, pour the beaten eggs and vanilla essence in the batter and stir well. Ensure no lumps are formed.

Step 4

Slowly add the Maida and mix well. Gently pour milk and mix until all ingredients are combined well. Take a baking tray and grease with butter and pour the mixture into it. Sprinkle some cashew nuts and raisins on top. You can add other dry fruits and berries to make this cake more delicious.

Step 5

Place the tray in a microwave oven and bake for 30 min or until the cake rises to the top and turns slightly brownish. To ensure that the cake is baked well by inserting a knife or toothpick, if it comes out clean, then your cake is ready to relish.

Step 6

You can also prepare this dish without a microwave by preparing it in a shallow pan by filling it half with sand. Place the tray with batter on it carefully and let it bake over medium flame.

Step 7

When the sand is heated through, keep the cake tin on top. Cover with a pressure cooker lid without gasket for 30 min. Insert a knife into the center and if it comes out clean, then the cake is ready. Remove, cool and cut into slices. Serve with a cup of tea or coffee.

Blueberry Cake Recipe

Ingredients:

- *1 cup blueberry*
- *1 tablespoon baking powder*
- *1 tablespoon vegetable oil*

Main Dish

- *1 cup milk*
- *2 egg whites*
- *1/2 cup apple juice*
- *1 cup cake flour*

Blueberry Cake Recipe:

Step 1

To prepare this delicious cake recipe, take a large bowl and add corn flour and baking powder in it, mix well.

Step 2

Take another bowl and beat egg whites in it with the help of an electric beater. Add these fluffy egg whites to the flour mixture and mix once again. Next, add apple juice, milk, and vegetable oil to the cake batter. Stir the mixture continuously.

Step 3

Take a baking dish and grease it with vegetable oil and pour the cake mix in it. Sprinkle crushed blueberries in the cake mix and place the baking dish in an oven.

Step 4

Bake the cake at 200° Celsius for half an hour. When done, take out the baking dish and allow it to cool on a wire rack. Then, carefully take out the cake with the help of a knives. Serve immediately

Blueberry Cupcake

Ingredients:

- 1 cup blueberry
- 1/4 teaspoon baking soda
- 2 drops vanilla essence
- 1/2 teaspoon baking powder
- 1 tablespoon butter

Main Dish

- *1 cup all-purpose flour*
- *120 ml milk*
- *1 egg*
- *1/2 cup sugar*

Blueberry Cupcake:

Step 1

To prepare this cupcake recipe, take a large bowl and add all purpose flour, baking powder, blueberries, along with baking soda, vanilla essence, sugar, butter and milk to it. Mix all the ingredients well.

Step 2

In another bowl, crack open the egg and beat well with an electric beater until fluffy. Add this beaten egg in the flour and blueberries mixture, and combine together to prepare a smooth batter.

Step 3

Take a cupcake tray, brush with butter and then pour the blueberry batter equally. Finally, place the cupcake tray in an oven for about 30 min and baked the cupcakes.

Step 4

After half an hour, bring out the tray and with the help of a greased knife, bring out the cupcake and serve when cool. (Optional: You can garnish the cupcakes as you like.)

Buckwheat Pancakes with Blueberry Sauce

Ingredients:

- 5 cup soya milk
- 2 egg
- 1 tablespoon canola oil/ rapeseed oil
- 2 cup jowar flour
- 5 teaspoon cinnamon
- 2 cup blueberry
- 2 tablespoon sugar free pellets
- 1 cup apple sauce
- 1 teaspoon vanilla extract
- 1 cup buckwheat

- *1 teaspoon baking powder*

- *3 tablespoons orange juice*

- *2 tablespoon arrowroot*

Buckwheat Pancakes with Blueberry Sauce:

Step 1

In a large mixing bowl, combine milk, apple sauce, eggs, vanilla extract and oil. Beat all the ingredients well and set aside. In a smaller bowl, combine the buckwheat flour, jowar flour, baking powder and 1 teaspoon cinnamon. Next, add the dry ingredients into the milk mixture, and mix all of them together.

Step 2

Heat oil in a skillet over medium flame and pour the pancake batter using a ladle and spread the batter evenly. Cook the pancake until it turns golden-brown on both sides. Then you can add more milk or small amount of water if you prefer a thinner pancake. Repeat the same steps with the rest of the batter and cook the pancakes. Place the cooked pancakes in a plate and set it aside.

Step 3

For the sauce, combine the orange juice, four teaspoons of cinnamon, blueberries, arrowroot and sugar free pellets in a small saucepan and place it over medium flame. Bring the ingredients to boil and then lower the flame. Simmer until a thick consistency is achieved. Remove from the flame and pour the warm sauce over the cooked pancakes and enjoy

Lemon Blueberry Tartlets

Ingredients:

- *1 cup blueberry*
- *1/2 tablespoon lime zest*
- *60 gm butter*
- *1/4 teaspoon vanilla extract*
- *3 tablespoons almond flour*
- *5 tablespoon lemon juice*
- *2 egg*
- *1 cup granulated sugar*
- *1 cup all-purpose flour*

Lemon Blueberry Tartlets:

Step 1

Take a deep bowl and add vanilla extract, butter, half cup sugar, 1 egg, almond flour and flour. Blend the mixture until the sugar dissolves. Then, beat the mixture until fluffy. Knead a dough from the mixture, cover it with cling film and refrigerate for 1 hour.

Step 2

When done, take out the dough and roll it. Using a cookie cutter, cut the circles out of the dough. Now, take a tray of muffin cup and place each dough portion on it. Press it with your hands to attach it firmly and prick with fork. Refrigerate for about 40 minutes. Meanwhile, preheat the oven at 180° Celsius. Then, bake the chilled tartlets for 15 minutes.

Step 3

To make the lemon curd, take a pan and add lemon juice, lemon zest and remaining half cup sugar in it. Over medium flame cook it until the sugar dissolves properly. Meanwhile, whisk the egg in a bowl and slowly pour the pan contents. Whisk and beat for a while and then sieve the mixture. Now, bring it to boil and when done, let it cool completely.

Step 4

Now, take the tartlets and pour the lemon curd and top up with blueberries and powdered sugar. Refrigerate until set and serve

Blueberry Muffin

Ingredients:

- *400 gm flour*
- *1 tablespoon baking powder*
- *1/4 cup sugar*
- *50 ml refined oil*
- *1 beaten egg*
- *0 salt as required*
- *150 ml milk*
- *3/4 cup blueberry*

Blueberry Muffin:

Step 1

Grease muffin cups or line with paper cups and set aside. Preheat the oven to 400°F (200c). In a medium bowl, combine flour, sugar, baking powder, and salt. Make a well in the center of the mixture and set aside.

Step 2

In a small bowl, combine beaten egg, milk, and oil. Add this mixture all at once to the flour mixture. Fold in blueberries and stir just until combined. Do not over stir.

Step 3

Spoon batter into prepared cups, filling each about two-thirds. Bake for 18 to 20 minutes or until golden. When a wooden toothpick is inserted near the middle, it should come out clean.

Step 4

Remove from muffin cups and let cool on a wire rack for 5 minutes.

Fruit Curd

Ingredients:

- *1 cup hung curd*
- *1/4 cup chopped strawberry*
- *1/4 cup blueberry*
- *1/4 cup crushed apple*
- *1 teaspoon Raisins*
- *2 teaspoon Honey*
- *1 chopped kiwi*
- *2 sprigs Mint Leaves*
- *1 teaspoon walnuts*
- *1 teaspoon almonds*

Fruit Curd:

Step 1

Whisk hung curd and honey.

Step 2

When fluffy, add chopped strawberries, kiwi, apples and blueberries. Mix well.

Step 3

Garnish with lots of walnuts, raisins and almonds and mint springs.

Step 4

Serve fresh and chilled

Eggless Whole Wheat Blueberry Cake

Ingredients:

- *2 cup blueberry*
- *1 teaspoon vanilla extract*
- *1/2 teaspoon baking soda*
- *120 ml canola oil/ rapeseed oil*
- *50 gm corn starch*
- *1/2 teaspoon salt*

Main Dish

- *150 gm wheat flour*
- *200 gm almond flour*
- *480 ml milk*
- *200 gm brown sugar*

Eggless Whole Wheat Blueberry Cake:

Step 1

To prepare this cake recipe, begin with pre-heating oven at 180° Celsius. Next, take a round cake pan and put parchment paper in it carefully.

Step 2

Now, take a large bowl and sift together almond flour, wheat flour, corn starch, baking soda, and salt. Mix all the ingredients well.

Step 3

Next, take an another bowl and add milk on it, canola oil and vanilla essence in it. Mix all of these ingredients well. Now, combine the flour mixture with the milk, and mix together to prepare the cake batter. Now, carefully add in the blueberries to the mixture.

Step 4

Then, pour this prepared mixture in the baking dish and bake it in the pre-heated oven for 50 min. Once done, allow the cake to cool at wire rack. Serve warm!

Hot Milk Cake

Ingredients:

- *1 cup milk*
- *2 teaspoon baking powder*
- *2 cup sugar*
- *4 egg*
- *1 teaspoon vanilla extract*
- *1/2 cup butter*
- *2 pinch salt*
- *2 cup all-purpose flour*

Hot Milk Cake:

Step 1

Take eggs and butter out of the refrigerator and keep them at room temperature. It is very important to have all your baking ingredients at room temperature for that perfect moist cake.

Step 2

Take a deep bottomed pan. Add the milk and allow it to boil. Now add the butter and melt. Mix well and remove from fire. Let it come down to room temperature.

Step 3

Add the vanilla extract to the milk and butter mixture. Meanwhile, break the eggs in a bowl and beat them vigorously. Add the sugar spoon by spoon and mix in the eggs till it is completely dissolved and the mixture in soft and fluffy with stiff peaks. The color this mixture should ideally turn to lemony yellow.

Step 4

Sift together the flour and baking powder and slowly add to the egg-sugar mixture. Use the cut and fold method and ensure that no lumps are formed in the process. Take small quantities of flour.

Step 5

Now add milk to this thick mixture of flour, eggs and sugar and add the salt. Beat well with a hand blender or with a fork or beater. Beating is important as this will help the cake rise. When you see air bubbles in the batter, it is ready to go inside the oven.

Step 6

Pre-heat the oven at 180° for ten minutes. Divide the batter into 2 greased and floured round cake pans Bake for about 30 minutes at 350 °F (175 °C).

Step 7

Cool on racks for 10 minutes (you may need to run a knife around the edge first) then turn out to cool. It is important to allow your cake to cool first or it may disintegrate if you try to take it out of the baking dish.

Step 8

Frost with icings of your choice or you can simply place some fruits on top and dust with icing sugar. This cake is ideally served with milk, tea and coffee.